AF351196

This book belongs to:

____

____

____

____

First published 2023 with an exclusive licence from the author to CHEETAH® Purrrrrrr Publishing, an imprint of CHEETAH® Toys & More, LLC (CHEETAH®).

Contact us: 1-860-781-1276, 1-876-909-6311 (WhatsApp),
info@mycheetahacademy.com; paulettetrowers@yahoo.com

ISBN 13: 979-8-3303-3425-4
ISBN 10: 8-3303-3425-4

Dear CHEETAH® family:

Our little books were specially created to help our early readers master their decoding skills and build reading fluency. The repetitive use of high-frequency words, word families, decodable words, rhymes, and vivid illustrations facilitates this process. Our stories complement the objectives and content highlighted in the Jamaica Early Childhood Curriculum Guide and the Ministry of Education and Youth Grade I National Standards Curriculum.

In journeying through our series, our little ones will develop a deeper awareness of, and appreciation for, our Jamaican culture. Our books also have universal appeal, as any early reader can identify with the characters, events and subjects in our texts. Readers will get to enjoy the stories, build vocabulary, and exercise critical thinking by engaging in the activities at the end of each story.

Additionally, as a precursor to our series, or as a support to it, we've created a decodable 'sentence strip' book for the very young readers and those who require more scaffolding.

Happy reading!

CHEETAH®

Chasing and capturing your dreams with you.

Letters are like the building blocks of a grand castle made of stories. Let's go! Let's build castles with words!

My decodable words:

Dad, glad, sad, tell, well, let, yet, sick, trick, bit, sit, Rob, sob

Letter sounds:

- consonant sound /s/ in the initial and final position in words
- long vowel sound /ā/ as in digraph 'ai'
- long vowel sound /ō/ as in digraph 'oa' and VCV pattern.

Word families: 'ad', 'ell', 'et', 'ick', 'it', 'ob'

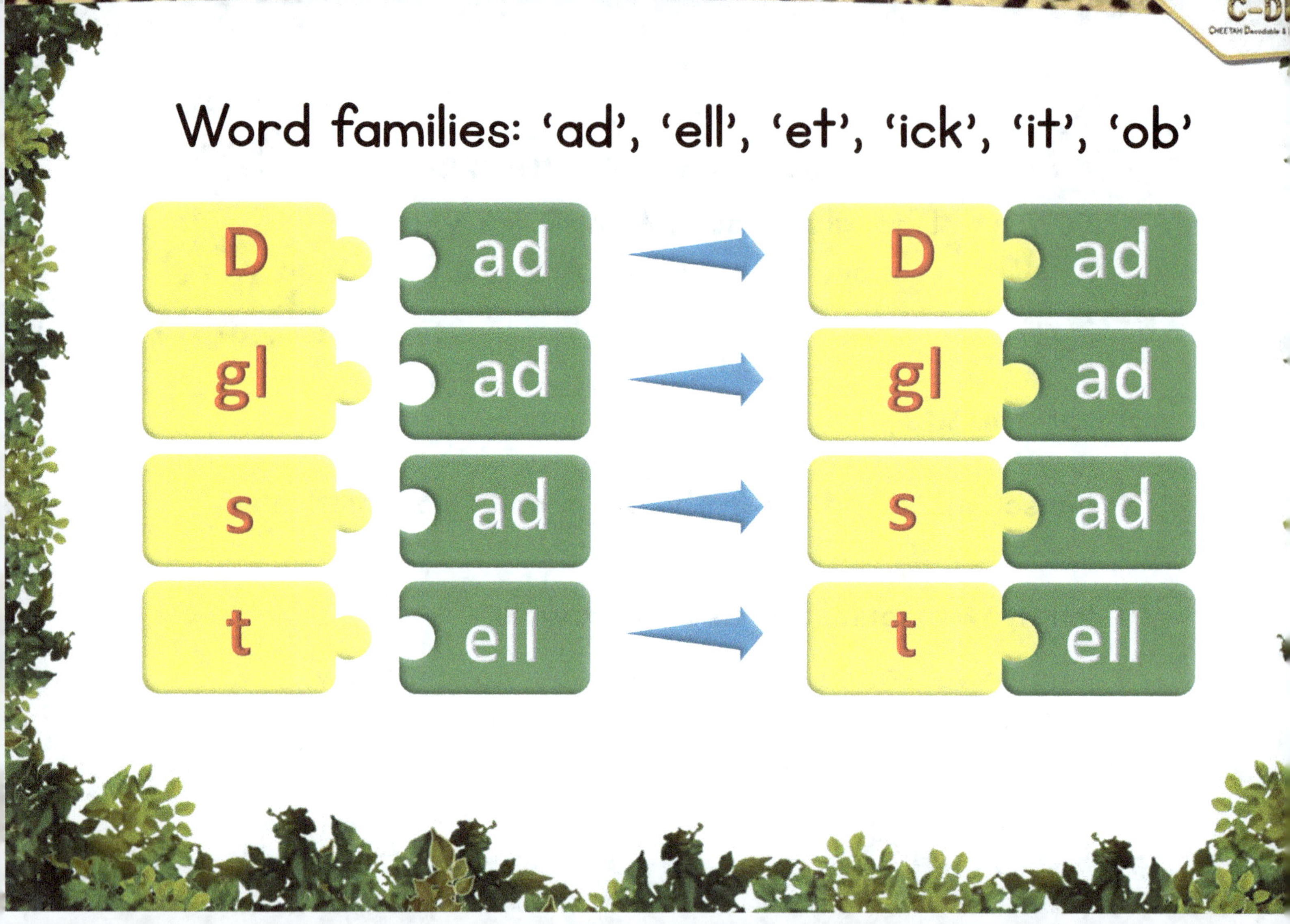

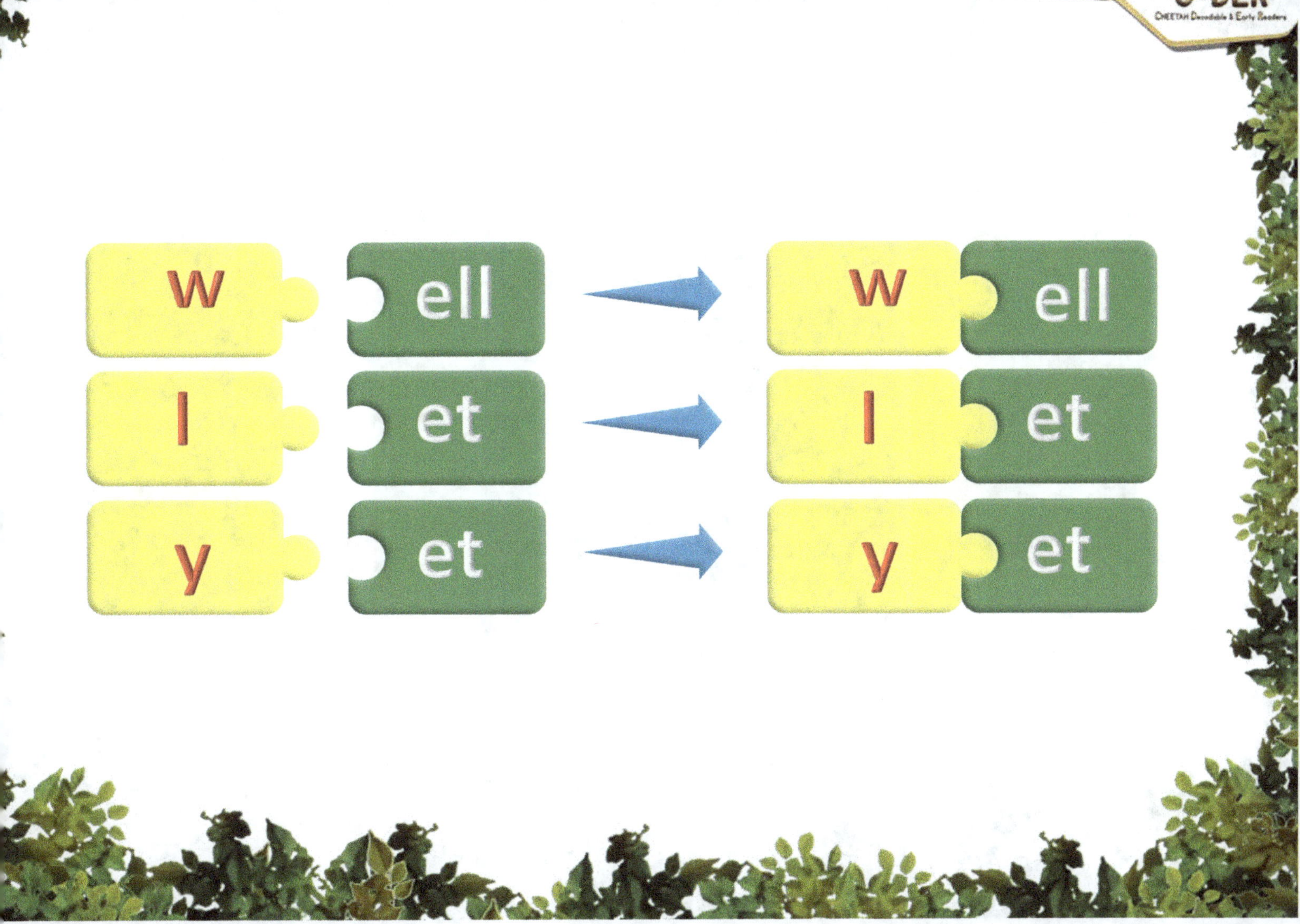

w
ell
l
et
y
et
w ell
l et
y et

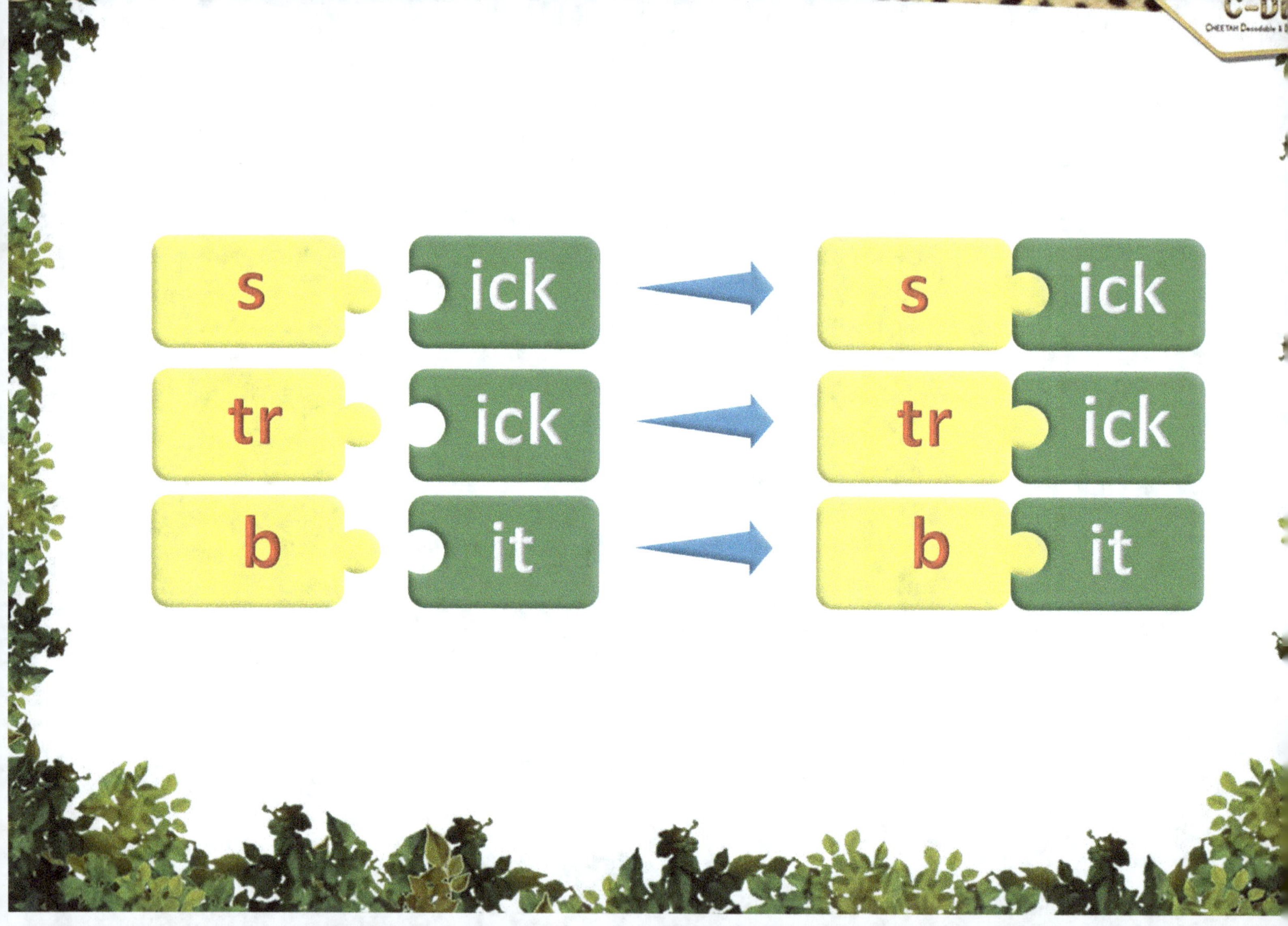

s
ick
s ick
tr
ick
tr ick
b
it
b it

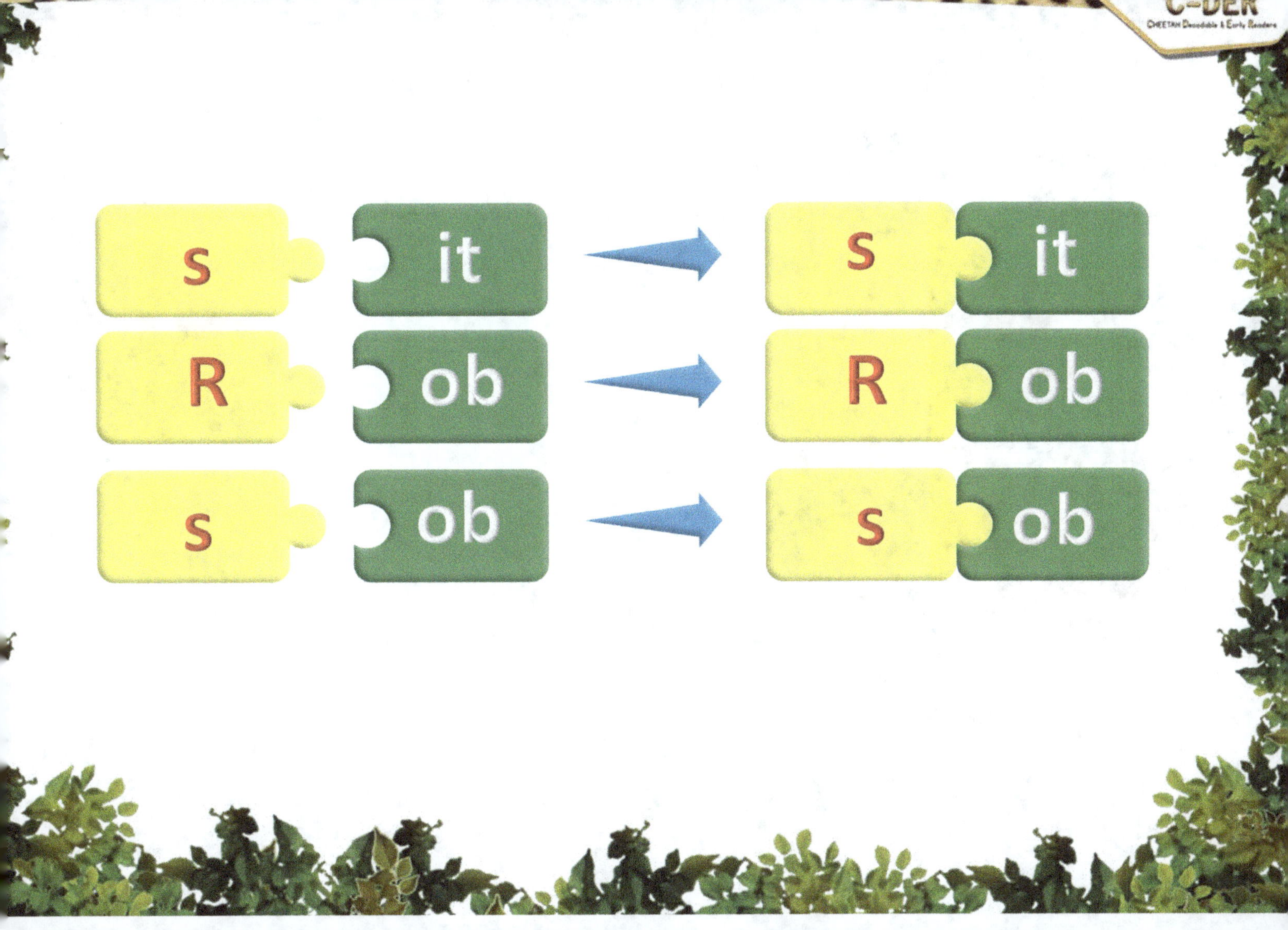

s   it
R   ob
s   ob
s it
R ob
s ob

C-DER
CHEETAH Decodable & Early Readers
wash your
1

Sam's Boat

'Dad, see my boat. It does not sail.

I put it in the big orange pail.

It does not stay up. It does not float.

Tell me what is wrong with my boat.'

3

Dad comes in. Sam starts to sob.

He wants to play with his friend, Rob.

'It is okay, son. Let me look at it.

You and Rob have to wait a bit.'

Wash
your

Dad takes the boat. The boys
are sad.

Sam asks, 'What is wrong with
my boat, Dad?'

'I do not know yet,' says Dad.
'Let me sit.

We will find out in a little bit.'

Dad sits and looks at the toy sailboat.

He wants to know why it does not float.

Why does it sink? It is made of wood.

Why does it not float as it should?

9

'Hmmm,' says Dad. 'Now, I see.
Come and see boys. Come here next to me.
I am sorry, Sam. Your boat is sick.
I can fix it. I know a trick.'

'Look, do you see the hole below?
I will plug it to stop the water flow.'
Dad puts some putty in the hole to plug it.
The boys have to wait a little bit.

11

After some time, the boys try
to sail.

They are happy that they do
not fail.

'Look, Dad!' calls Sam. 'Come
see my boat!

See how well my boat can
float.'

13

Dad comes and looks and he is glad.

The boys are playing. They are not sad.

'Thank you, Dad,' says Sam. 'My boat is not sick.

It is well again. Thanks for doing that trick.'

Discussion and activities:

1. Ask the children whether they have ever been in a situation where something belonging to them was damaged and needed fixing. Have them share how they felt in this situation and how the problem was solved.

2. Have the children identify the words with the target letters and sounds.

3. Have the children make the sounds of the target letters and identify rhyming words in the text.

Discussion and activities:

4. Discuss the words: sob, putty and plug as used in the context of the story.

5. Have the children read the text aloud.

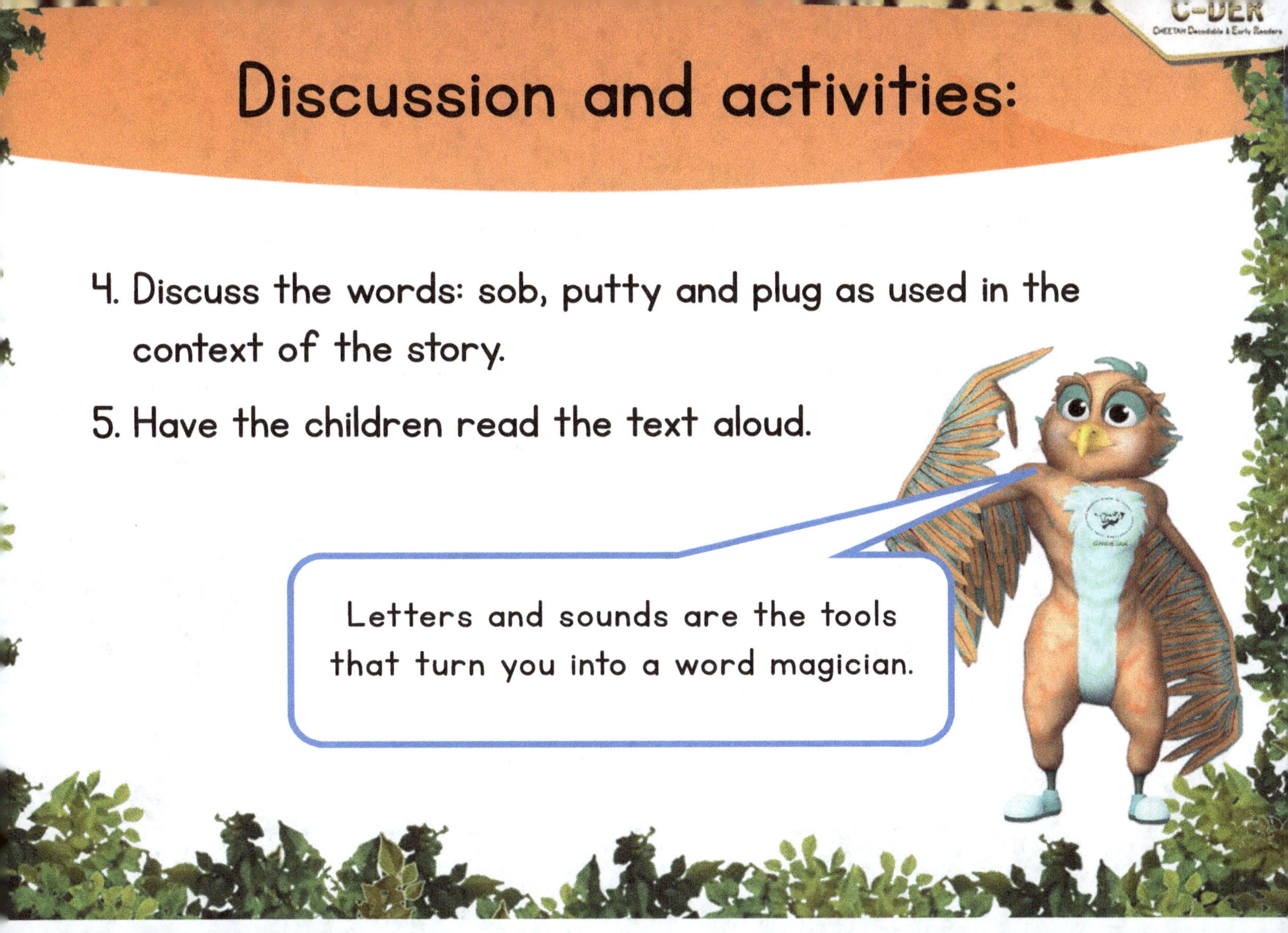

Questions:

1. What did Dad mean when he said that the boat was sick?

....

2. What 'trick' did Dad do in the story?

....